Why Make Yourself Crazy?

100 Ways to Rid Your Life of Needless Stress

G. Gaynor McTigue

Why Make Yourself Crazy?
100 Ways to Rid Your Life of Needless Stress

ISBN 0-9716427-0-2

Printed in the United States of America

Introduction

Why make yourself crazy? Aren't you dealt enough stress in life without having to heap more of it on yourself? Yes, *you* are the likely cause of much of the anxiety, pressure and hurriedness you experience every day. You might balk at this, given that most of life's complications appear to be beyond your control. But if you look you at them honestly—and that's the key—you'll realize how unnecessary many of your daily frenzied activities, deadlines and crises really are.

It's time to stop the insanity and take back control of your life. Starting today. Starting now.

This book can help you reclaim a more enjoyable, relaxed and enriching existence in much the same way it was lost—inch by inch, on the multiple battlefronts of your life: work, home, family, personal finances, relationships, health, nutrition, community, leisure, and many other areas of involvement.

The concepts in this book aren't profound. In fact, they're disarmingly simple. *Why Make Yourself Crazy?* offers 100 basic, put-it-right-to-work strategies for eliminating chaos, stress and frustration from your life. The mere act of reading the book can be liberating in itself. But that will be short-lived unless you commit yourself to making each applicable strategy a permanent part of your life. And that requires frequent rereading, reeducating and reminding yourself—until the long-term benefits of a calmer, happier existence take hold and become ample inducement in themselves. The tone of the book is frank and direct—at times scolding. The intention is to mimic your own inner voice, exhorting you to slow it down, do it right, stop making everything more complicated than it is.

As the author of *Life's Little Frustration Book*, *You Know You're Middle Aged When...* and *How Not To Make Love To A Woman*, I am a veteran chronicler of the many ways we tie our lives into knots. I have also been an active participant. There is no lunacy set forth on these pages I have not been guilty of myself, and no strategy I have not employed to address it. I personally can attest to the peace and sense of well being you'll gain by gradually working these changes into your life.

If you find this book works for you, please recommend it to others. The fewer people there are to swim upstream against, the easier our own efforts will be. And perhaps someday, through our example, we can even turn the tide.

G. Gaynor McTigue

1

Do one thing at a time.

Do it mindfully. Do it well. Enjoy the satisfaction. Then go on to the next thing. Multitasking might work for computers, but humans have yet to get the hang of it. It leads to careless mistakes, shoddy work and unreliable performance. Worst of all, having to do things over. This is no way to live. Give what you're doing your undivided attention. Take the time to get it right. And enjoy the experience.

Why make yourself crazy?

2

Throw something out every day.

You've got too much stuff in your house. Office. Garage. Attic. Useless clutter that's weighing you down, getting in the way, obscuring the things you really need. Be realistic. If you're not going to use it, lose it. And you don't have to make a humongous project out of it. Every day, find one thing you don't need and toss it. Or give it away. Over time, the clutter will begin to vanish and space and order will magically appear in your home... and your life.

Why make yourself crazy?

3

Have small, intimate get-togethers.

Big parties are expensive, time-consuming and a heck of a lot of work. Even if you're lucky enough to talk to everyone, it may only amount to brief, cursory snippets of conversation. Big bashes can be fun, if you're not the one throwing it. Smaller parties are easier to arrange, less work, less expensive, and leave lots of time to enjoy your guests, who feel more special, too. Entertain fewer people...more often.

Why make yourself crazy?

4

Please, get the amount of sleep you need.

You can't cheat sleep. What you don't get in rest you'll pay for in diminished alertness, poorer performance, drowsiness, and irritability. And you'll have to make up your sleep debt anyway! Get into the habit of knocking off early (there are few things in life that can't wait till tomorrow), get a good night's sleep (generally about 8 hours), and start the day rested, refreshed and ready to do your best.

Why make yourself crazy?

5

Make changes in your life gradually.

No crash diets. No sudden, intense workout programs. No radical overhauls of who and what you are. You might maintain it for a while, but it can't last. True change takes lots of small, mindful, subtle decisions over time that add up to bigger, more enduring transformations. They're less disruptive to you and everyone else, and inevitably get the results you want. Be patient. If you're really intent on change, you should develop the staying power to achieve it without having to act rashly. Do it by degrees.

Why make yourself crazy?

6

Entrust responsibility to responsible people.

There are those who always have a convenient excuse for not getting it right, showing up late, or botching the job entirely. And there are those who consistently, efficiently and unequivocally come through for you. This isn't luck. It's responsibility. Not something you're born with. Something you do. Responsibility takes effort. Concern. Pride. And perseverance. Who do you want to entrust your children, your home, your finances, and your other important responsibilities to? Lose the whiners and stick with the winners.

Why make yourself crazy?

7

Don't carry the world upon your shoulders.

So the song goes. And how true. There's enough crime, starvation, wretchedness, injustice, depravity and evil out there to drag us into utter despair every day...if we choose to let it. Do yourself a favor. Don't. Recognize that there's little most of us can do as individuals to make wholesale changes in the world. But within the sphere of our own lives, there's plenty we can do. Try kindness, generosity, understanding, and love. Starting with your own family and working your way out. And guess what? When you add up these individual contributions from all of us, it *can* make a difference in the world. So take care of the local stuff and the rest will follow.

Why make yourself crazy?

8

Get into shape.

Lack of time is no excuse for not exercising. In fact, being in shape will improve your physical and mental capacity to such an extent, you'll probably *gain* time. And enjoy life more. A regular fitness routine, combined with good eating habits, will keep you leaner, healthier, more energetic. You owe that to yourself. And your family. Being in poor physical condition only adds to your stress and the sense of futility that you'll never catch up. Climb out of that swamp. Get fit. Feel good.

Why make yourself crazy?

9

Speak up.

Don't know what they're talking about?
Ask. Don't agree with what's being said? Speak up.
Your opinion is just as valid as anyone's. And the
only stupid question is the one that's not asked.
People often assume we have the same prior knowl-
edge they do, and start in the middle of things.
It's not your fault, it's theirs. So before it goes any
further, interrupt. Tell them to backtrack a bit.
Ask basic questions. And get up to speed.

Why make yourself crazy?

10

Eliminate meaningless deadlines.

Our life is full of them. Arbitrary and unrealistic time constraints imposed by ourselves and others that serve only to make us more pressured, anxious, stressed out. For no worthwhile reason. Avoid the trap of assigning time frames to everything you do, especially if you have little idea how long it will take. Instead, make your goal one of completing a project in a careful, professional, satisfying manner. In other words, as long as it takes to do it right. Save your nerves, and your energy, for the few *real* deadlines we face...like April 15th.

Why make yourself crazy?

11

If your kids can't play together nicely, separate them.

How many times do you need to go in and scold your kids for fighting and squabbling? Only once, if you play it smart. When they can't get along, separate them. Deny them the privilege of each other's company until they can work out a peaceful solution. It will make them appreciate each other more. And will give you a needed break. So when the kids start going at it, divide and conquer.

Why make yourself crazy?

12

Don't view life as cyclical.

It can make it seem dull, routine and predictable. And it's not. Instead, view your life as a straight line stretching off toward the future. What's to come has never happened before. Even holidays and traditions can be refreshingly different if you make them so. Prejudging the way things will play out only contributes to their sameness. Surprise yourself. Shed your jaded notions and resist falling into the same tired thinking patterns that rob your life of vitality and diversity.

Why make yourself crazy?

13

Accept that people think differently than you do.

You could spend your entire life trying to win over people to your point of view. The simple truth is, you won't. At least, not everyone. Even if you present the most logical, rational, airtight arguments, some people will never see it your way. Maybe they're proud, stubborn, stupid, or in some instances–did you ever stop to think?–*right*. Don't waste your time trying to convert the diehards. Instead, work with them, live with them, respect their differences, and be thankful the world isn't full of people exactly like you.

Why make yourself crazy?

14

Take frequent breaks.

There's no glory in drudgery. Nor is it fun or satisfying. Break up tedious assignments into smaller tasks. Pause and get away from the work periodically. Insert other lighter activities in between. Each time you come back you'll feel fresh and energized. And before you know it, your project will be finished.

Why make yourself crazy?

15

Be prepared.

Nothing succeeds like thorough preparation. It makes you more efficient and productive, gives you confidence, and minimizes anxiety and doubt. Prepare yourself for the *unexpected,* too, and you'll be better able to deal with it. Things often play out chaotically because people just aren't ready. Do you want your life to be a litany of rushed, slapdash, unpredictable, loose-ended episodes? Or smooth, well-planned, fully satisfying outcomes? Then be prepared.

Why make yourself crazy?

16

Don't eat it if you don't want it.

The restaurant serves oversized portions. You take more food than you can eat. You don't want to disappoint your host. You don't like leaving leftovers. You feel guilty throwing food away. Whatever the reason, you often end up eating far more food than you want...or need. This stresses your system, adds unwanted calories and leaves you bloated and full. Don't always feel you have to finish it. In fact, leave the table a little hungry. Overeating can lead to many problems.

Why make yourself crazy?

17

Keep like things in like places.

Don't store the tennis rackets in the closet and the balls in the garage. Or the vacuum cleaner in the basement and the bags in the attic. It's hard enough to find one thing much less remember where two or even three items are kept. And it's more work fetching them. Store related items together so you'll know exactly where they'll be.

Why make yourself crazy?

18

Take the back roads.

Yes, it will take more time, but the trip will be fun, relaxing and enjoyable...and thus go faster. Back roads offer one-of-a-kind sights, interesting people and unique local ambiance, while high-speed superhighways drone on with the blandest scenery and tedious driving. Not to mention those cloned service areas. Make getting there a learning, enriching experience. Stop often. Explore. And arrive safe and refreshed.

Why make your self crazy?

19

Don't be goaded into making hasty decisions.

If you feel unsure, or don't know enough to make a decision...*don't*. Most decisions can be put off. Wait till you have all the facts. And never be rushed into deciding by a salesperson because a "special offer" will expire. Any reputable company will extend their terms until you've at least had time to think about it–something they may not want you to do. Don't agree to anything you aren't sure of.

Why make yourself crazy?

20

Look for that secret cashier.

Somewhere in the store there's a little-used cash register, service desk or courtesy desk that will also ring up your purchases. You just have to find it. People naturally drift toward the busiest lines. Take a moment to seek out that alternative checkout. You might be surprisingly rewarded.

Why make yourself crazy?

21

Accept that life can be awkward at times.

No matter how carefully you plan things, or imagine they'll turn out, or believe they're supposed to be...some events will leave you confused, uneasy or out of kilter. And you can't explain why. Maybe it's your mood, the alignment of the planets, the weather, your physical condition...or a combination of things. In any case, accept these messy, awkward occasions as part of life. And have faith that things will soon fall back into sync. And you know they will.

Why make yourself crazy?

22

Give things a chance.

Today, everyone expects instant results. So there's a tendency to give up on things too soon—the book you're reading (hopefully not this one), the mutual fund you've invested in, the musical instrument you're learning, the person you're dating. Don't be so quick to abandon something that doesn't give you immediate results. This could prevent you from experiencing the greater benefits that may emerge if you stick it out longer. Be patient. Give it more time. Find out for certain if something is worthwhile rather than make a hasty departure.

Why make yourself crazy?

23

If every morning is a mad dash...*get up earlier!*

How often we hear the complaint "I never have enough time in the morning." Duh...*make* time. Simply wake up earlier. Leave yourself ample time to dress, eat a nutritious breakfast and get off to where you're going...sanely. It will set a composed, rational pace for the entire day. Break the insidious cycle of rushing by retiring early and getting up early, with a good night's sleep in between.

Why make yourself crazy?

24

Don't delay your happiness.

People will fritter away their entire lives waiting to be happy. For them, happiness is always just around the corner–sure to happen when they finish school, get a job, find a spouse, have kids, get the kids out of the house, claim their inheritance, retire... You'll never be happy that way. Experience happiness now, from within, by appreciating the gifts and accomplishments you're already blessed with, rather than waiting for some elusive external event or acquisition to take place.

Why make yourself crazy?

25

Don't try to know everything.

You *can't* know everything. So focus on what you need to know, what you're curious to know, and what will help make your life easier, happier and more productive. Don't feel pressure to learn things other people know but have little relevance to you. It's not a competition. There are probably lots of things you know that they don't, but do you hold it against *them*? Keep your quest for knowledge focused and selective.

Why make yourself crazy?

26

Don't over-volunteer.

Resist volunteering for more than you can handle, more than your free time allows. Volunteering is great, but heavy involvement can steal important time from your family and relationships. (And it shouldn't be used as an excuse to avoid more important obligations.) If the work becomes too demanding, simply say no. Nobody else is going to look out for you better than yourself. If we all "volunteered" to spend more time with the kids, visit our parents, make loving homes, and carve out special time for ourselves, there wouldn't be a need for so much volunteering in the first place.

Why make yourself crazy?

27

Steer clear of negative people.

You know them well: the whiners, the ones who find fault with everything, who always lay a hard luck story on you, who constantly give you grief over harmless trifles, or make wholesale denunciations of people, institutions and cultures that don't suit their fancy. Unless you're stuck with them, shun them. They'll pull you down, darken your outlook, try to make your life as miserable as theirs. Who needs that? And if you are stuck with them (relatives, coworkers, house mates) don't agree or encourage them. In fact, say nothing and leave the scene whenever they launch into one of their diatribes.

Why make yourself crazy?

28

Take long vacations.

At least two or three consecutive weeks, more if you can swing it. Don't be chained to your job by the belief you're indispensable or the company will fall apart while you're gone. We all need an extended break. It takes at least a week to unwind and acclimate yourself to leisure. By the time the fun really begins, most people are headed back to work. Don't deny yourself the extended vacation you really deserve...and desperately need.

Why make yourself crazy?

29

Don't watch the local news.

It's usually a visual rap sheet of murders, fires, rapes, and rip-offs. With a few boring parades and awkward, uninspired banter between the anchors mixed in. Local news blows the negative way out of proportion, and that can make you fearful, depressed, a prisoner in your own home...leaving you with the distorted view that the world is going to seed. Hey, it's not all that bad out there. Silence the doomsayers. Turn off the TV, go out and have a good time. Good news is rarely reported, the bad news will find you.

Why make yourself crazy?

30

Run through it again.

Don't always assume another person is on the same page as you are. Or fully understands what the program is. Repeat the instructions, go through the itinerary once again, ask that phone numbers and directions be read back to you. Better to be redundant (or a pain in the butt) than have everything screwed up altogether.

Why make yourself crazy?

31

Take naps.

This may run counter to today's misguided work ethic, but several studies have found that people are more productive (and undoubtedly more pleasant) when they take afternoon naps. A twenty-minute to half-hour siesta can work wonders, and it shouldn't interfere with your night's sleep. Darn the naysayers. Close the door, have a pleasant snooze and reap the benefits.

Why make yourself crazy?

32

If you don't want to answer the phone...don't.

There's no law or rule of etiquette that says you have to drop what you're doing, interrupt a meal, lose your train of thought, or miss your favorite show...to answer the telephone. Unless you want to. If not, screen your calls with caller ID. Or let your voice mail pick it up. There are few things that can't wait until you're available to talk. And you certainly don't want to be waylaid by an endless yapper. Busy? Let the phone ring.

Why make yourself crazy?

33

Don't buy what you really don't need.

Before you buy anything, ask yourself two questions. One: do I really need this? And two: could I put this purchase off another week, month, year? If you're honest with yourself, you'll be surprised at how many purchases you can delay or avoid altogether; even better, how much money you can save. And you'll realize how perfectly well you can get along with what you already have.

Why make yourself crazy?

34

Get over it.

So you're late. You lost the game. You got a spot on your suit. It cost $350 to fix the car.
Will it make a whit of difference a year from now? A week from now? Stop agonizing and get on with it. Factor in these disruptions as a part of life, not exceptions to it. As opportunities to respond to adversity. And if they don't happen, it's gravy.

Why make yourself crazy?

35

Don't live and die with the financial markets.

If you've invested long-term—and have no intention of cashing in soon—ignore the day-to-day fluctuations of the market. They'll have little bearing on the final tally, but will exact a costly toll in dashed hopes or inflated expectations every time the market dives or soars. Don't become a ticker-tape junkie. Forget about your investments, like gold socked away in a vault.

Why make yourself crazy?

36

Don't feel guilty losing touch with people.

You could spend the rest of your life trying to keep up with all the people you've grown close to over the years. Nice if it was possible, but unnecessary and impractical. Accept that those you no longer associate with, or have moved away, will soon fall out of your loop. As undoubtedly you will theirs. And that's okay. Perhaps someday you'll get together. Perhaps not. In any case, at least you'll have each other's memories. So don't be down on yourself, or fault the other person, for drifting apart. It's only natural.

Why make yourself crazy?

37

Read more books, fewer periodicals.

It's the difference between noshing on snack foods and sitting down to a good, healthy meal. Newspapers and magazines provide snapshots and summaries–pieces of information that offer immediate satisfaction and value, but whose usefulness soon fades. Books, on the other hand, give us the bigger picture–a deeper understanding of humanity and long-term intellectual nourishment. They're also wonderful escapes. Kick the info-glut habit and benefit from the enduring wisdom of great books.

Why make yourself crazy?

38

Don't worry until you have something to worry about.

Maybe you're the type of person who, when things are going great, begins to fret some unforeseen calamity will come along and spoil it. Or– when someone doesn't arrive on time, or something doesn't happen on schedule–you immediately think the worst case scenario. Or maybe there's *always* some fear and worry lurking in the back of your mind. Whatever the case, think of the thousands of times your worrying has proven unwarranted. The overwhelming odds are, this time will have a happy ending, too. Relax, enjoy your life and for crying out loud stop worrying.

Why make yourself crazy?

39

Don't buy what you already have.

This may sound obvious, but there are probably several duplicated items in your home right now... *and you don't even know it.* Especially if you tend to accumulate a lot of clutter (see #2 on how to get rid of it). So before you go shopping, check to see that you don't already have what you think you need (the rear of the refrigerator, cabinets and closets are good places to start). Make a list of infrequently used possessions and where they're kept. Over time, you can save a lot of money just by keeping track of what you've already got.

Why make yourself crazy?

40

Don't always feel you have to be doing something.

There's nothing wrong with doing nothing. In fact, it wouldn't hurt to set aside time each day to do just that. *Nothing*. Sit and relax. Or take a stroll. Block out all the clutter in your mind. And then let it wander. At first, you may become anxious thinking of it as downtime–wasted moments when you could be accomplishing something. But guess what? You *are* accomplishing something. You're grabbing the reins of a runaway team of horses and pulling them back into an easy, manageable pace. You're freeing up your mind. Getting control of yourself. Learning that living is not just doing...but being. Cut yourself some slack now and then and enjoy some good, salutary nothing time.

Why make yourself crazy?

41

Keep the menu simple.

When entertaining (hopefully in small gatherings: see #3), there's no need to overwhelm your guests with more choices than necessary. (Why make *them* crazy?) An hors d' oeuvre, a main dish, a couple of side dishes and dessert is plenty. It will save you time and money, and make entertaining easy enough that you'll want to do it more often. Overdoing it also unfairly raises the stakes for guests who want to reciprocate. Focus on the quality of what you serve, not the quantity, and on making your visitors feel comfortable and welcome. Your get-togethers can't help but turn out special.

Why make yourself crazy?

42

Get all the facts first.

Don't be so quick to judge, accuse or jump to conclusions before all the facts are in. It can hurt you, and it can hurt others. Get the full story—all sides of it—from reliable sources before you pass judgment. Society has developed a lynch-mob mentality, ready to pounce on anyone or anything the minute a rumor takes hold, and is sadly unrepentant when proven wrong. Don't you be a part of it.
Get the facts before you act.

Why make yourself crazy?

43

Improve your vocabulary.

It's frustrating not knowing what a word means, thinking it means something else, or having to ask people to explain it. If you don't know the definition of something, look it up. Strive each day to learn a new word, how to pronounce it and how to use it. Adding to your vocabulary helps you grasp immediately what the world is communicating, rather than grope around for meaning and clarification.

Why make yourself crazy?

44

Call in your kids' restaurant orders before you arrive.

If you have small, antsy, unruly, or especially hungry children (or, God forbid, all of the above), call in your order before you leave the house. By the time you get there, are seated and settled, the food will soon arrive to grab and hold their attention. Trying to keep young kids entertained and in their chairs is a task. So call ahead, cut the wait and maybe you can even enjoy the experience.

Why make yourself crazy?

G. Gaynor McTigue

45

Work close to where you live.

Even out of your home, if feasible. You might make more money schlepping a distance, but in the long run, is the extra pay worth the lost time with your family, the high commutation expenses, and the wear and tear on you? Probably not even close. Get a job near your house. Simplify your lifestyle. Be home for dinner. Watch your kids grow up.

Why make yourself crazy?

46

Do things off-peak.

Unless you love crowds, jostling and waiting in line, try to get things done when everyone else isn't. Go to the bank, cleaners, supermarket and pharmacy during slow periods. Eat at restaurants later or earlier than the hoi poloi. (You might even be rewarded with an early-bird special.) Vacation during fringe seasons when it's less crowded and a lot cheaper. (Pulling younger kids out of school shouldn't hurt them, especially if you work educational activities into the vacation.) In other words, live conveniently and affordably off-peak.

Why make yourself crazy?

47

Don't forget to breathe.

Sure, breathing is automatic. But measured, lung-filling, stress-reducing breathing is not. Make a conscious effort to take a deep breath or two every so often, especially during ticklish and trying moments of the day. It'll relax and replenish you, relieve some of the stress and leave you better able to deal with a tense situation. Claim the air you need to succeed.

Why make yourself crazy?

48

Don't try to replicate past events.

They'll rarely be as good as the first time around, and more likely disappointing. Instead, strive for fresh experiences that in themselves will one day become poignant memories. Why try to recapture the past when you already have it?

Why make yourself crazy?

49

Sleep on it.

Time and your subconscious are excellent decision makers, editors, problem solvers, and healers. So when it's late, and you're tired and perplexed, simply go to bed. Let your mind do the work while you're enjoying a good night's sleep. Chances are, you'll awaken to a better answer, a brighter outlook, a clearer understanding of what to do.

Why make yourself crazy?

50

Bored? Shake up your routine.

Your day doesn't always have to follow the same lackluster script. Break out of your dull routine and experience life in fresh new ways. Maybe it's eating breakfast out, taking a different route to work, reading a section of the newspaper you never do, visiting a store or attraction you normally pass by, revamping your style of dress, modifying the way you treat or interact with others. Each is nothing earth-shattering in itself, but it affirms the power you have to make things happen, to change your perspective, to inject excitement and diversity into everything you do. Break the monotonous regimens of your life.

Why make yourself crazy?

51

Learn to listen.

Don't merely pay ear service...carefully *listen* to what people are saying to you. Make a conscious effort to hear and understand every word they speak. Resist the urge to interrupt, and wait till the speaker has finished completely before responding. Don't miss key parts of the message because you're thinking of something else, or prematurely forming your response. And be sensitive to implied or hidden meanings behind the words—that is, what the speaker is *really* trying to communicate. You'll be amazed at how much more you'll learn and understand when you truly listen.

Why make yourself crazy?

52

Be persistent.

Don't be put off, shunted aside, delayed, or denied because someone else doesn't want to do his job, or fulfill her obligation, or perform their responsibility. Be persistent, stand your ground and get what you're entitled to. Refuse to accept partial, less-than-adequate or vague responses to things you have a right to know, or services you're paying for. Sometimes it's easier and less confrontational to give in, but that only leads to anger, stress and frustration. And encourages people to take advantage of you and those who follow you. Keep them honest; demand satisfaction.

Why make yourself crazy?

53

Get off the upgrade treadmill.

Products like computers, software, TVs, cars, stereos, telephones, and skis don't change as fast and dramatically as their makers would like you to think. They'll pull out the stops to convince you that what you have now is passé or obsolete (even though they recently sold it to you!). Don't buy it. If the item serves your main purpose, and serves it well, keep it. A few additional bells and whistles, or a marginal increase in performance, isn't worth the extra expense and hassle.

Why make yourself crazy?

54

Create a mud room.

Or a mud area. A transition place where
weathered footwear and outer garments can be
shed, along with the day's travails and concerns.
A comfortable space where you can warm up or
cool down and avoid tracking in unwanted dirt
and moisture. A mud area will keep your home
cleaner and more orderly, while leaving just one
small space to tidy up.

Why make yourself crazy?

55

Store things out of the way.

Take an extra moment or two to put things back where they belong. Why? Because you can bet that wherever you put them temporarily they will soon be annoyingly in the way. More than that, things left out tend to multiply to the point where work surfaces and living space soon disappear. Nip those stragglers in the bud and haul them out of sight.

Why make yourself crazy?

56

Research your purchases.

Get objective reviews of products and services from consumer magazines, Internet sites, message boards, friends, and relatives whose opinions you respect. You'll soon get a valid consensus of which products are right for you, and which to avoid. And don't use a lack of time as an excuse for not doing research. You'll spend lot more of it, and money too, if you have to replace an item that turns out to be a dog. Get it right the first time.

Why make yourself crazy?

57

Confirm your appointments.

Will your friend remember your lunch date?
Will your flight take off on schedule? Will the
repairman you've taken a day off from work to
let in show up? Don't leave yourself guessing.
Or worse, empty-handed. A one-minute phone call
to confirm the event can save you a lot of grief
later on.

Why make yourself crazy?

58

Recognize when you've attained "enough".

One of the weaknesses of our culture is not stopping, or even knowing, when we've achieved enough. Which leads to excess, exhaustion, egotism, insatiable appetites, and damaged relationships. Learn the point at which you've worked enough, rested enough, spoken enough, eaten enough, drank enough, exercised enough, complained enough, and beaten your opponent enough. Know when you've accumulated enough possessions, taken on enough debt, received enough praise. In recognizing these limits, you can eliminate the lack of fulfillment and sense of futility we feel when we can never achieve "enough".

Why make yourself crazy?

59

Don't forget the little projects.

In our efforts to concentrate on the big kahunas of our life–work, school, family, relationships–we often forget to service the smaller needs: minor repairs and upkeep, organizing cluttered living spaces, catching up on paperwork...in general the everyday maintenance of our lives. Overlooked, these things can pile up, get in our face, detract from our quality of life. Actually, these lesser projects can offer us refreshing breaks from major pursuits. And keeping pace with them will impart a sense of order and satisfaction, that things are under control. So take care of the little stuff, too.

Why make yourself crazy?

60

Always have a trip planned.

Whether it's a weekend jaunt or a world tour, the mere act of planning a future vacation is liberating, uplifting and exciting to look forward to. And you don't even have to spend money to start the process. Read up on places you'd like to go, send away for brochures, block out the time, and begin enjoying the wonderful benefits that travel offers...before, during and after. Always have an escape planned.

Why make yourself crazy?

61

Write it down immediately.

Before you forget, jot down the name of that restaurant, the person you're supposed to call, the time of the next practice, the great website you heard about...whatever useful information has just been given you. Chances are, with everything else cramming your brain, you'll otherwise forget it. That's why a palm-size computer or electronic assistant is always a good thing to have handy. Don't miss out. Write it down.

Why make yourself crazy?

62

Give good, unused clothing away.

In your closet right now there's clothing you've hardly worn. How about that mistake purchase you made but are too proud to admit it? Maybe it's a garment you're waiting for to come back into style, a size you're hoping you'll one day to fit into again, or clothes you've just grown weary of. Chances are–be honest–you're never going to don any of this attire again. So rather than clutter up your closet, give it to someone who could really use and appreciate it.

Why make yourself crazy?

63

Eat slowly.

A meal is a gift, a source of pleasure, a time to relax and replenish. So why diminish the experience by scarfing it down like it may be your last? This may take some doing, but get into the habit of eating slowly. Chew deliberately and savor each bite. Take frequent pauses. Give your body a chance to accept and digest the food, rather than shocking and overwhelming it. And try not to think about finishing fast so you can get to something else. *This* is what you want to be doing. So give each repast the enjoyment and sociality it deserves.

Why make yourself crazy?

64

Be more forgiving of people.

Don't be poised to jump all over someone the minute they make a mistake or don't deliver exactly what you want. People can't read our minds. Nor do they always perform flawlessly. (Do you?) If someone is really trying, cut them a break. Save the eye-rolling, peevishness and complaints for when it's really justified, not just as a stock reaction to every minor glitch that befalls you. Be realistic and build the likelihood of human error into your expectations.

Why make yourself crazy?

65

Stop worrying about your age.

Forget about the number of years you might be racking up. Your age has more to do with what you eat, how much you exercise and what your approach to life is than mere chronology. Worrying about it will only add to that feeling of agedness you're laying on yourself. Time is going to advance inexorably no matter what you do. Fortunately, you have power over how it will or won't affect you. Use that power.

Why make yourself crazy?

66

Make waiting worthwhile.

Cussing, fretting and agonizing never made waiting go any faster, and actually prolongs it. But using that downtime productively will. So when you're stuck in traffic, far back in line, or waiting for someone to show up...think of these moments as opportunities, not obstacles. Review and fine tune your plans for the day. Observe the world around you for its beauty, interest and ideas. Or just take a deep breath, relax and enjoy this unplanned time to yourself. In other words, turn what you normally might treat as a setback into an advantage.

Why make yourself crazy?

67

View paying bills as a positive experience.

This may be a real stretch for many since bills can be a great source of aggravation, fear and anxiety. But it doesn't have to be that way. Rather than receive your invoices with dread, let them be reminders of what you're paying for: products that improve your life, services that keep you safe and comfortable, and good times you've enjoyed.

Be thankful when you have the funds to satisfy your obligations and view these payments as accomplishments, not diminishments. Look at a bill paid as a transaction resolved, a milestone reached, a responsibility met.

Why make yourself crazy?

68

Adjust your clothes to the ambient temperature.

Why keep your overcoat on in a stifling department store? Or spend time in the chill outdoor air without a jacket? Putting on or peeling off as needed will help you stay comfortable, perform better and enjoy the activity you're involved in. Wear layers that allow you to adjust to the environment. Take advantage of coat checks and lockers. Bring along an extra garment just in case (like tying a sweater around your waist). And don't let what others are wearing, or not wearing, pressure you into the wrong attire. Dress intelligently. Live comfortably.

Why make yourself crazy?

69

Try not to attach money to self-worth.

Yes, most people do to some extent. After all, our self-esteem is buoyed by our achievements, and money can be a quantifiable measurement of achievement. But accumulating money for its own sake is an unquenchable pursuit that will always leave you less than fulfilled. It also diverts your attention from nobler, more selfless acts. Know the point at which trying to earn more becomes superfluous, even detrimental, and direct your efforts to worthier pursuits that offer lasting satisfaction.

Why make yourself crazy?

70

Discipline rationally, not angrily.

Don't wait until you're furious before disciplining your kids. By then you'll be too worked up to apply any constructive punishment...and more likely to shout, hit and even abuse. Instead, reprimand bad behavior early on, before it, and your reaction to it, get out of hand. The kids can then learn from the discipline, and you'll save yourself untold aggravation and regret by remaining calm and in control.

Why make yourself crazy?

71

Take responsibility for your own life.

It's easy to blame family members, coworkers, governments, and everybody else when things don't go right for you. In fact, pointing the finger has become one of the more unattractive traits of our society. Don't hide behind a litany of excuses and accusations; instead, take responsibility for the choices and decisions you make. The sooner you do, the sooner you'll be able to recognize your mistakes, correct them and move on to better things.

Why make yourself crazy?

72

Never throw the same party every year.

People will grow to expect it. In fact, they won't schedule anything else in anticipation of it. They'll even be ticked off at you if you decide one year not to have it. Or be hurt, thinking they weren't invited. Repeat parties grow stale, predictable and all blur together—like you never really left the last one. Better to throw one-of-a-kind celebrations that carve out unique, lasting memories.

Why make yourself crazy?

73

Do what needs to be done first...first.

This should be automatic, but for many reasons, we'll put off more important and pressing things to take care of lesser priorities first. Not only does it leave that bigger thing hanging over us, it often deprives us of the time and energy we'll need to accomplish the important task. Every morning, take a few moments to consider what project would make most sense to get out of the way first. Then meet it head on, without becoming sidetracked, without trying to squeeze something else in between. Then go on to the next most critical...and watch the stress ease away.

Why make yourself crazy?

74

If it's broke, fix it.

Nothing gets more neglected than minor repairs. They can stare us in the face for years. But letting them wait robs you of more than full use of the item involved. Things like sighing toilets and wobbly garden gates eat away at your sense of order and serenity. Get into the habit of taking care of it right away. Just making an appointment with the repair person will ease your mind (unless of course the guy doesn't show). Even more satisfying, fix it yourself. Upkeep is as good for the mind as it is for the home.

Why make yourself crazy?

75

Don't pay before the work is completed.

No matter whom you're hiring–painter, service technician, caterer, contractor–hold back the last installment until the work is finished to your satisfaction. That way you'll still have leverage if there's a problem. Take away the monetary incentive and you're inviting shoddy work, delays, loss of interest, and an unfinished job. No matter how nice and well-intentioned your vendor may seem, avoid paying it all up front.

Why make yourself crazy?

76

Don't lend out books.

Unless you want to be rid of them. You'll never get them back. You'll forget whom you lent them to and when. Then, when you go to look for one, you won't have a clue where it is. Books are one of those items, like borrowed money, people neglect to return. Tell them it's available at the library.

Why make yourself crazy?

77

Don't be so self-conscious.

Most people aren't judging you. In fact, they're usually so wrapped up in the business at hand, or in their *own* image, they're barely noticing what you're wearing, how you're coming off, or that everything isn't just so. To prove it, think how easily you dismiss (or don't even notice) the minor flaws of others in light of their bigger, more positive traits. Being self-conscious needlessly distracts you from your larger purpose. Accept that your presentation will always have imperfections. They actually make you more human, more likable. Lighten up, be natural.

Why make yourself crazy?

78

Expect people to cancel out on you.

Last-minute dropouts and no-shows can be disappointing–especially when you've gone to a lot of trouble. Blame it on our over-scheduled times, a general slackening of social responsibility, whatever. But this, unfortunately, is the way things are. So be ready for it. If you're planning an event or activity involving several people, expect one or more will almost certainly cancel. Invite or recruit extra people to make up for the inevitable loss. And if everyone does show up (slim chance), you'll enjoy an unanticipated bonus.

Why make yourself crazy?

79

Note where you set things down.

Make a deliberate mental snapshot of where you temporarily put that pen, tool, pair of reading glasses, or piece of paper. Not easy, since it's usually a distraction that made you set it down in the first place. But after a few tries you'll get the knack of remembering where it is. Also, avoid bringing a tool or item you're working with unnecessarily away from the work area. It will usually be unwittingly left behind. This simple advice can save you hours of search time over the course of a year.

Why make yourself crazy?

80

Let the store assemble it.

It's tempting to think you can save a few bucks assembling that gas barbecue, play set or bicycle yourself. (Or maybe you just love exasperating, time-consuming tasks.) Save yourself the anguish. Let someone who can practically do it in his sleep assemble it. Faster, better and cheaper in the long run. And you won't suffer the despair of learning at one o'clock in the morning that a key part is missing, or you put it together backwards.

Why make yourself crazy?

81

Stop and think.

It's amazing how much time, money and trouble we could save ourselves if we just took time to think before we acted. Run possible scenarios in your mind. Weigh consequences. Consider alternatives. Ask more questions. Or just think it through. You'll be surprised at how often you'll overrule your initial rushed impulses and find a better way. Just by taking the time to think. Your mind is the most efficient tool you have. Use it.

Why make yourself crazy?

82

Don't equate saving with buying things on sale.

Real saving takes sacrifice. Doing without.
And putting money away. But we've been deceived,
or are deceiving ourselves, into thinking we're
saving money by spending it. That's why everything
is almost always on sale. (Which makes you suspect
it's overpriced to begin with.) So when they tell you
to act now or lose out on big savings, don't buy it.
Wait until you really need the item. Chances are
you'll find it on sale anyway. Why keep chasing after
so-called "savings" that just put you further into
debt?

Why make yourself crazy?

83

Speak clearly and deliberately.

Avoid these barriers to good communication: rushing your words to the point where they lose their meaning or effectiveness; talking around a problem rather than getting to the point; unnecessarily repeating yourself or saying far more than you need to. Instead, choose your words carefully, take the time to express yourself clearly and distinctly, and speak with directness and honesty. If another tries to step on your words, or steer you in another direction, calmly hold your ground until your point is made. You listen to others. It's only right they listen to you.

Why make yourself crazy?

84

Take ten minutes a day to neaten up.

Supplement your regularly scheduled cleaning by spending a short time each day neatening your home. Use those few minutes to clear a cluttered surface, tidy a child's room, clean out a drawer, throw out a useless item or two, dust a long-forgotten place, put something away...or whatever obvious need is staring you in the face. You'll be surprised at how much this small attention to neatness can accomplish over time. And how organized and productive you'll become. And when you do get around to more intense cleaning, the job will be that much easier. Take ten minutes a day to tidy up.

Why make yourself crazy?

85

Don't believe for a minute...

...you'll get the number of servings the recipe says you will...you can perform a complex computer task with a single click of the mouse...your call is important to them...the "push here on red" button will get you across the street any faster...you're indispensable to your company...your cake will look anything like the one illustrated on the box...the battery will last anywhere near what they claim... Get smart. Lower your expectations.

Why make yourself crazy?

86

Indulge in a pair of good, comfortable slippers.

Few things can be more welcoming, more unburdening, when you return home. Keep them near the door, so you can quickly shed your constraining day shoes and relax. Get a pair that slips off easily when you want to put your feet up. And make sure they're sturdy enough to wear when putting out the garbage. A pair of slippers is like a old friend. Comfortable, relaxing and forgiving. Invest in a pair.

Why make yourself crazy?

87

Play with the kids as soon as you get home.

Yes, you have a million other things to do. Or maybe you'd just like to relax. But spending time with your kids first will show them you love them above all else. It will satisfy their need to be with you, and preempt both their nagging and your putting them off. Chances are, they'll soon get distracted anyway and go off to do something else, leaving you with time to yourself...without guilt. Make a fuss over the kids first.

Why make yourself crazy?

88

Start with a clean work surface.

Before you begin a project, first clear your desk, kitchen counter or work area of the clutter that will surely get in the way. Then take out and organize the implements you'll need to get the job done, leaving yourself ample room to maneuver. That's it. The minute or two it takes to do this will save you considerable time and aggravation over the course of the project. Clear the decks first.

Why make yourself crazy?

89

Know when to go with a pro.

It's very satisfying when you can complete a project yourself, without having to resort to professional help. And that's great. But there are some projects–either because they're too complex, dangerous, extremely messy, or require several people–you should simply stay away from. Know what they are. Before you take on a task that may be out of your league, talk to others who have undertaken a similar project and learn from their experiences. Or read up about it. It could save you untold time, trouble and misspent effort.

Why make yourself crazy?

90

Take it to the next level.

When something goes wrong, try to avoid getting mired in the usual reactions of anger, frustration, disappointment, and despair. Instead, hoist yourself to another level—one of understanding, acceptance and fortitude. Say to yourself: *Yes, this is tough, but if I can meet the challenge and get through it—and I will—not only will I have dealt with this problem, I will be that much stronger to tackle an even worse crisis should one come along.* Sure, it's not easy. But if you ratchet up your reaction to strife a notch or two, and meet it squarely, you'll come out of it in much better shape.

Why make yourself crazy?

91

Don't say it, do it.

Boasting about the wonderful things you're *going* to do for yourself and others can actually be your *un*doing. For one, now you're expected to do them. Secondly, if you don't do them you appear weak, unreliable and irresponsible. If you really want to impress people, don't reveal what you intend to do...but simply do it. They'll be surprised and pleased with your accomplishment, and even more moved by your modesty. And if for some reason you can't get it done, no one will be the wiser.

Why make yourself crazy?

92

Ask what's involved.

Before you agree to take on a responsibility, sign up for a program or volunteer your time, determine the full extent of what's involved. It's only reasonable to ask questions up front, and withhold your participation until you've had time to evaluate your role. This may spare you a lot of regret later on. Don't be so quick to jump into the water before you know how deep it is.

Why make yourself crazy?

93

Store things in labeled or see-through containers.

Do you have any idea how much time is squandered, and energy spent, opening containers, boxes, bags and wrappers over and over just to find out what's in them? Why make every trip to the closet or refrigerator a scavenger hunt? Take a moment to label things prominently before you put them away. Or simply go transparent with see-through wraps and plastic containers.

Why make yourself crazy?

94

See the humor in things.

Life can be very funny. But if you're constantly stressed out or harried, you can miss much of the fun going on around you. Why deny yourself this delightful and rejuvenating aspect of life? Try to remain in good spirits even when confronted by aggravating circumstances. Laugh at your mistakes, and encourage others to laugh at theirs, too. Humor is contagious, and a readiness to laugh an endearing and beneficial quality. A little laughter can go a long way toward lightening up a business meeting, easing a tense relationship or getting you through a trying time. Have a good chuckle.

Why make yourself crazy?

95

Open the closed doors of your life.

A closed door is: *I can't do that. That's not me. I'm too old. It's too late. I'm too busy. I don't know enough about it. They won't take me seriously.* Nonsense. Remove these artificial barriers to greater joy and accomplishment. Cross the threshold to enriching new experience. Make the investment in time and effort to rise above the dull routine of your life to develop new talents, forge new friendships and strike out in new directions. The only real obstacle is you. Recognize this. Just open the door (there are no locks) and walk through.

Why make yourself crazy?

96

Give gift certificates.

Finding a gift that someone doesn't already have, or fits properly, or suits their tastes...can be a daunting task. So why even go there? It's a lot easier—and just as appreciated—to purchase a gift certificate from your recipient's favorite store, restaurant or service and let *them* decide. People rarely get the chance to buy something special for themselves. They'll enjoy the experience...and the self-selected gift you'll get credit for. You'll also avoid the awkwardness and fake enthusiasm for gifts that miss the mark. Present a gift that's sure to succeed.

Why make yourself crazy?

97

Expect it to take longer and cost more.

Whatever it is—a home improvement, a new appliance, a vacation, a repair, a recipe—it's our human nature to underestimate how long it will take and how much it will cost. So rather than set yourself up for a nasty surprise, start high, think worst case scenario, and fully expect it to be more than you initially thought it would be. And if for some incredible reason it isn't, it's like getting a bonus. Hope for the best but don't count on it.

Why make yourself crazy?

98

Don't fret over looming, stressful events.

You have to undergo a medical procedure, give a speech, meet your future in-laws, fire your assistant, fly on an airplane, compete in an important game. Fretting about it will only make you live through a negative outcome over and over...before it even or ever happens! Block out those bad thoughts and dwell on the overwhelming odds that everything will turn out just fine. (Even if you do lose the game.)

Why make yourself crazy?

99

Use the proper tools.

Nothing can get the job done better, faster, safer and ultimately more economically than the right tool. Buy, rent or borrow, but make sure you avail yourself of the benefits and convenience of quality tools. Take the time to learn how to use them properly and safely. Renting can be cheaper in the short run, but buying often doesn't cost that much more, and you'll almost certainly use that tool again...and again. Get it done like a pro.

Why make yourself crazy?

100

Take stock.

Every once in a while, lay in bed a few extra minutes, or stop whatever you're doing, and take stock of where you are. Think of your accomplishments, the obstacles you've overcome, the mistakes you've corrected, the blessings you've been given. Be thankful for your good health and the loved ones in your life. This doesn't mean you should rest on your laurels, but at least give yourself some credit for how far you've come. So periodically take a mental inventory of everything good in your life... and don't let current troubles cloud your greater achievements.

Why make yourself crazy?

Order here for additional copies of
Why Make Yourself Crazy?

Why Make Yourself Crazy? makes an excellent gift. It's also a fitting give-away for group functions and special events, or a premium for marketing promotions. To order additional copies, complete this form and mail with your credit card information, or a check made payable to Pick Me Up Books.

Quantity	Price per copy	Total
_____ X	$9.95 =	_____

CT residents add 6% sales tax   _____

Add shipping & handling ($2.00 for first book, $.50 for each book thereafter)   _____

Total remitted: _____

Discounts for quantities of 10 or more copies available.
Email: sales@pickmeupbooks.com

Name   Please print clearly:

Organization

Address

City   State   Zip

Charge to: ☐ **MasterCard**   ☐ **VISA**   ☐ **Amex**

Card number   Exp. Date

Signature

Make checks payable to Pick Me Up Books.

Mail to: Pick Me Up Books, PO Box 321013 Fairfield, CT 06432

Or fax to: 203-254-7791

Also by G. Gaynor McTigue

Life's Little Frustration Book   St. Martin's Press   ISBN 0-312-95215-5

You Know You're Middle Aged When...   Pinnacle Books   ISBN 0-7860-0066-X

More Life's Little Frustration Book   St. Martin's Press   ISBN 0-312-96098-0

How Not To Make Love To A Woman   Dove Books   ISBN 0-7871-1031-0

About the Author

G. Gaynor McTigue is the author of five books, including *Life's Little Frustration Book* and *You Know You're Middle Aged When...*, whose combined sales have surpassed 100,000 copies. His books have been featured on hundreds of radio and TV shows nationwide.

Mr. McTigue has also written numerous articles and essays that have helped millions of people improve the quality and enjoyment of their lives. His work has appeared in major city newspapers and national magazines, among them the *Los Angeles Times, New York Daily News, Chicago Sun-Times, The Philadelphia Inquirer, The Boston Globe, The Miami Herald, Travel Holiday Magazine, Advertising Age,* and others.

For several years Mr. McTigue wrote a weekly column for America Online and hosted a celebrity chat show. He is a member of the American Society of Journalists and Authors (ASJA).

G. Gaynor McTigue is available for media interviews, speaking engagements and book signings. He can be contacted by email at: jerrym321@aol.com